I0555086

MINDFUL MENSTRUATION
A Practical Guide to Menstrual Cycles and Mental Health

Joanna Greenbaum, M.A., LMFT

CONTENTS

the honest truth

I didn't really understand my period until I was in my late twenties.

An acupuncturist, who happens to be a man, explained to me what was happening in my body each month. He wasn't mansplaining, he was educating me. He was honoring my body and helping me connect with it. And he did so without any judgement that I didn't already know this information.

Around that time, I started to learn more. I read books, listened to podcasts, downloaded apps. It was like putting a puzzle together - it all made sense.

As recommended by a mentor, I began tracking my cycle daily - specifically by hand. After a couple months there was a shift. I was understanding my body more and understanding my mental health in a new way.

While tracking is not a cure from the ups and downs of menstruating, it has made the process significantly more tolerable. Just by being more mindful of cyclical changes there has been a huge opportunity to better understand and support myself. I am more connected, more in tune, more compassionate, and more free.

My journey continued in graduate school as I studied clinical psychology. With no mention of the menstrual cycle in any of my classes, I found myself seeking out coursework and research studies on my own.

As I began to share what I had learned I started to hear personal stories from people about their periods. It became clear most people want to understand their body and their cycle more. I now am focused on educating others and normalizing conversations about menstruation.

Everyone has their own story about their cycle. Whether it be about their first period or their most recent one, there is so much to explore within our own individual experiences.

I wrote Mindful Menstruation to help others better understand their cycle and do so from a place of compassion. Consider this guidebook part of your story of how you got to know your period better. I also invite people who don't menstruate to read this book to deepen their understanding of partners, family members, and friends.

The content in this guide was developed to make menstrual education more accessible. There are many wonderful books already published on the topic, I have included some recommendations at the end of this book. Please consider Mindful Menstruation as a "Period 101" introduction and know there is much more information out there if desired.

The design and content of this book was informed by coursework, publicly accessible research studies, published work (cited where relevant), and anecdotal experience.

Please note, research on the topic of menstrual cycles and mental health is always being further informed as more research is funded and published.

If you remember one thing from this book, I hope it is that people who menstruate are cyclical beings, not linear ones. We are meant to ebb and flow, to recharge, to slow down, and to begin again.

Joanna Greenbaum
Marriage and Family Therapist
Certified Menstrual Cycle Coach
@inflowwithjo

made for you

Intentions of this guide:

- Provide education you may not have gotten when you were younger

- Reframe shame and negative perceptions of menstruation

- Highlight the intersections of menstruation and mental health

- Help you mindfully embrace your cycle and live in more harmony with your body

Important things to remember:

- Periods are nuanced, they are never exactly the same

- Consider this guide and tracker a place to connect with yourself in a private and personal way

- This guide is a foundational introduction to the topic of menstruation, if you have questions or concerns about your cycle please schedule time with a health professional for individualized care

PART I

LEARN THE CYCLE

menstrual cycle 101

Society tells us we should be
growing every day. That we
should all strive for daily
improvements where we appear
noticeably better, faster,
stronger, happier, more
productive.

While this is a wildly high
expectation for anyone, it goes
against the natural cyclical
rhythm of the menstruating body.
For someone who menstruates,
life is not linear.

We do not feel the same every
day because we are not the same
every day.

Purpose of a menstrual cycle

The menstrual cycle is a recurring cycle that is centered around the goal of reproduction. Throughout the cycle, hormones change in support of developing and releasing an egg and increasing the uterine lining for potential pregnancy. If an egg is not fertilized the uterine lining is shed during the days of menstruation.

Not all women bleed
Not all who bleed identify as women

There are many times in life when someone may not get a period such as during pregnancy, while breast feeding, due to certain health issues, or while using various methods of hormonal birth control.

Additionally, menstruation is not synonymous with gender. For some their menstrual cycle may deepen connection with gender while for others having a cycle may contrast connection with their gender identity.

Cycle length and period length

While cycles generally occur an average of every 28 days, the timing of them is always an individualized experience (ex: 24 days for some, 32 days for others). The length of a cycle can vary throughout a lifetime and can shorten with age. In addition to cycle length, one may also notice their period length which can range on average between 3 to 7 days of menstruating.

Irregularity of cycles and periods can occur at any age and is especially common during adolescence and during perimenopause. It is good to share irregularity with a doctor to ensure there isn't an underlying issue.

Life stages and cycles

One's relationship with their cycle can change throughout their life. When learning about your cycle it's good to check in with what's currently happening between you, your cycle, and your life stage.

Additionally, some may struggle with issues such as PCOS, fibroids, endometriosis, or infertility that can cause emotional and/or physical pain at various points in their life. Many have also gone on and off hormonal birth control, have gone through the experience of miscarriage, abortion, or pregnancy which all can greatly impact emotions, mental health, and one's relationship to their body.

menarche, average age 12

Menarche (men-ar-key) is the first occurrence of menstruation, in this time it can take a while for adolescents to have a "regular" period

on-going cycles, teens-20s-30s

Someone who menstruates will experience on average of over 400 cycles throughout their lifetime

perimenopause, average age mid-40s

Before menopause, the body starts the transitional process of perimenopause which can last on average four years

menopause, average age 51

Menopause is reached when someone goes 12 consecutive months without a period

postmenopause, average age 50s

After reaching menopause one may still experiences menopausal symptoms, but these generally subside after a few years

Four phases within one cycle

Each phase has its own purpose and function. The four phases in order are: Menstrual, Follicular, Ovulatory, and Luteal. These phases can be thought of as on-going transitions that we are always moving through.

The challenge here is to embrace the sometimes uncomfortable changes that occur across phases. Associating seasons* with phases can be helpful to remember and appreciate the essence of each phase.

Phase	Event	Season*	Theme
Menstrual	*Shedding the uterine lining from last cycle (when one bleeds)*	*Winter*	*Hibernation, Recharging*
Follicular	*Egg prepares for ovulation*	*Spring*	*Newness, Starting over*
Ovulatory	*Egg released from the ovary to uterus*	*Summer*	*Opening up, Connection to others*
Luteal	*Egg could be fertilized and implanted or cycle continues to period*	*Fall*	*Winding down, Connection to self*

The "Inner Seasons" is a concept developed by Alexandra Pope and Sjanie Hugo Wurlitzer

Wurlitzer, S. H., & Pope, A. (2017). Wild Power: Discover the Magic of Your Menstrual Cycle and Awaken the Feminine Path to Power. Hay House, Inc.

Embracing the whole cycle

Getting to know the phases can help you connect with your cycle, not just with your period. An emerging term you may hear is "cyclical living" which implies living in flow with your cycle throughout each phase.

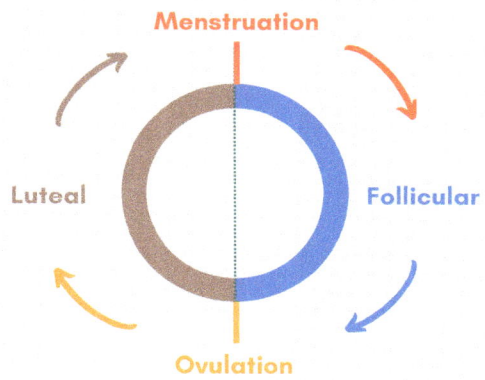

Noticing bio markers

In addition to noticing changes in mood and energy levels, biomarkers such as cervical mucus consistency, daily morning body basal temperature, or hormone levels through home urine tests can be tracked at home. Cervical mucus is a visual biomarker to notice and see changes (dry and sticky in the beginning and end of the cycle versus wet and slippery around ovulation.)

*The follicular phase is technically the first half of the cycle that encompasses your period and ovulation. When tracking it can be thought of as the time between menstruation and ovulation.

12

a deeper look into cycle phases

People are usually most aware of
the premenstrual and menstrual
phases. These phases often
involve physical and emotional
discomfort which leads people to
be more easily be aware of them.

My challenge to you is to start
to become aware of all the
phases. As with the rest of life,
it can be harder to recognize
what feels good over what feels
bad. Take note of what you
experience as nourishing. Some
moments may feel joyful, some
hours may feel energizing, some
days of solitude may feel
restorative.

The following framework outlines
common experiences among those
who menstruate. It is important
to remember that common
experiences do not mean they are
true for everyone. As you start
to notice aspects of your own
cycle, please remember it is okay
if you experience emotions
different than what's on the
page.

Menstrual phase

Symbolic season: Winter
Think: Hibernation, boundaries, recharging
Timing: Beginning of cycle
Number of days: Average 3–7 days

Function
The first full bleed is considered "day 1" of the cycle. Menstruation is when uterine lining sheds from the previous cycle.

Key Hormones
Estrogen low, Progesterone low

Cervical Mucus
Mixed with period blood during this time

Common Experience
Lowest energy levels. A time for personal reflection and evaluation. Tendency to have more social boundaries up. Focus on self care.

How to lean into this phase
Remember, this is a time to rest. Your value is not tied to productivity, it is okay to slow down. Trust this time for evaluation of your wants and needs.

Follicular phase

Symbolic season: Spring
Think: Newness, starting again, optimism
Timing: First half of cycle
Number of days: Average 14 days

Function

Starts with menstruation and ends after ovulation. Hormones begin to rise to prepare egg for ovulation.

Key Hormones

Estrogen rising, Follicle stimulating hormone (FSH) and Luteinizing hormone (LSH) rising

Cervical Mucus

Dry, sticky

Common Experience

Energy starts to rise. Openness to new things. Stronger ability to think big picture. A little more social. Sometimes the spike in energy in this phase can show up as anxiety for people.

How to lean into this phase

Embrace having your energy back, but remember you don't have to go from 0 to 100. You can ease back in after menstruation.

Ovulatory phase

Symbolic season: Summer
Think: Energy to get out, open up, connect
Timing: Midcycle
Number of days: <1 day for ovulation, phase average 3 days

Function
Ovulation is when the ovaries release an egg. Before the egg is released, cervical mucus can keep sperm alive for up to 5 days, a natural way the body increases opportunity for pregnancy.

Key Hormones
Estrogen, Follicle stimulating hormone (FSH) and Luteinizing hormone (LSH) all peak to highest levels, Testosterone present before ovulation

Cervical Mucus
Slippery, wet

Common Experience
Most energetic time. Strong communication skills. Peak confidence. Most social time. More open to receiving from others. Increased sex drive. Can feel lonely if isolated during this time.

How to lean into this phase
Remember this energetic high is temporary. Stay in the present, enjoy the company of others, and try not to burn out.

Luteal phase

Symbolic season: Fall
Think: Winding down and starting to get cozy
Timing: Second half of cycle
Number of days: Average 14 days

Function

After ovulation, estrogen decreases quickly and progesterone starts to slowly rise. Uterine lining continues to build, and the body prepares for either pregnancy or menstruation.

Key Hormones

Progesterone rises and is the dominant hormone, Estrogen first dips and then rises a little during this time.

Cervical Mucus

Dry, sticky

Common Experience

Energy declines. Possible irritability. Motivated to finish projects and tie up loose ends. Desire to nest at home. Less social. Easing into self care. Increase in appetite due to body's need for more calories in this phase. Decreased sex drive (if having sex, it may feel nice to take it slow.)

How to lean into this phase

Your emotions are valid even if they are amplified and uncomfortable. Avoid discounting your underlying emotions "just because you are PMSing." Get curious about what is below the surface and ask for alone time or support if desired.

getting familiar with symptoms

What happens for one person
during their cycle may look very
different for another. Knowing
your cycle and your symptoms can
help empower you to find your own
flow.

Please note similar to the
previous section, the signs and
symptoms listed here are
considered common, however they
are not universal nor are they
necessary to experience. Some of
these symptoms can be a sign of a
health issue, others can be
attributed to nutritional
deficiencies, sleep deficiencies,
being out of sync with the
natural circadian rhythm, over
exposure to endocrine disruptors,
dysregulated nervous systems,
and/or high levels of stress.

These lists are meant to help
provide language for cyclical
changes you might notice in your
daily life. If you have a
different experience than what is
on the page, please note it,
honor it, and get curious about
it. If you have questions or
concerns please consult a medical
or mental health professional for
appropriate care.

Common signs and symptoms
Follicular + Ovulatory

Mood/Emotions
- ❏ Less fluctuation in mood
- ❏ Less difficult emotions
- ❏ Increased confidence
- ❏ Playful, joyful
- ❏ Less sensitive
- ❏ Easier to access optimism and think about the future

Energy/Sleep
- ❏ Energized, possible adrenaline
- ❏ Increased motivation
- ❏ Less fatigue
- ❏ Need less rest
- ❏ Easier time exercising

Cognitive
- ❏ Increased concentration
- ❏ Easier to retain information
- ❏ Easier to make decisions

Appetite
- ❏ Decrease in food cravings
- ❏ Decrease in appetite

Menstrual

Follicular*

Ovulatory

Luteal

The follicular phase is technically the first half of the cycle that encompasses your period and ovulation. When tracking it can be thought of as the time between menstruation and ovulation.

Physical
❏ More comfortable in body
❏ Less bloating
❏ Less oily scalp
❏ Improved skin, less acne
❏ Easier digestion

Relational
❏ Openness
❏ Less stubborn
❏ Less sensitive to others
❏ Seeking connection
❏ Desire for social interaction
❏ More attracted to others
❏ Increase in libido
❏ Sadness, frustration, or disappointment may surface if there is a desire to be with others but you are alone

Mental Health
❏ Pre-existing mental health symptoms may be more stable (for example: OCD, ADHD, depression, anxiety, etc.)
❏ Potential change in anxiety levels, feeling keyed up or on edge, adrenaline, excess energy, feelings of burnout
❏ Potential change in depressive symptoms
❏ Potential decrease or absence of self harm thoughts or suicidal thoughts

If you are in crisis, please reach out for mental health crisis support:
SAMHSA's National Helpline, 1-800-662-HELP (4357)
National Alliance on Mental Illness, Call 1-800-950-6264 or Text "Helpline" to 62640

Resources above are for the United States, if outside of the country please reach out to local mental health support.

Common signs and symptoms
Luteal + Menstrual

Mood/Emotions
- ❑ More in touch with emotions
- ❑ Mood swings
- ❑ Desire for solitude
- ❑ Less ease accessing joy
- ❑ Ability to access difficulty emotions otherwise suppressed (anger, aggression, irritation)

Energy/Sleep
- ❑ Low motivation
- ❑ Moving slower
- ❑ Change in productivity
- ❑ Tiredness, Fatigue
- ❑ Clumsiness
- ❑ Hypersomnia or insomnia
- ❑ More vivid dreams at night

Cognitive
- ❑ Poor concentration
- ❑ Brain fog
- ❑ Forgetfulness

Appetite
- ❑ Specific food cravings
- ❑ Increased appetite

Menstrual

Follicular

Ovulatory

Luteal

Physical

☐ Tiredness
☐ Migraines or headaches
☐ Bloating
☐ Constipation, diarrhea
☐ Nausea, vomiting
☐ More frequent infections (yeast infections, UTIs)
☐ Dry vaginal tract

☐ Painful intercourse
☐ Breast tenderness
☐ Night sweats
☐ Hot flashes
☐ Acne, dry or oily skin

Relational

☐ Increased sensitivity
☐ Defensiveness
☐ Stubbornness
☐ Avoidance of social interaction
☐ Less attraction to others
☐ More self conscious
☐ Decrease in libido

Mental Health

☐ Worsening of pre-existing mental health symptoms (for example: OCD, ADHD, depression, anxiety, etc.)
☐ Hopelessness
☐ Anxiety
☐ Depression
☐ Keyed up or on edge
☐ Self harm thoughts or suicidal thoughts

If you are in crisis, please reach out for mental health crisis support:
SAMHSA's National Helpline, 1-800-662-HELP (4357)
National Alliance on Mental Illness, Call 1-800-950-6264 or Text "Helpline" to 62640

Resources above are for the United States, if outside of the country please reach out to local mental health support.

a brief hormone overview

While we get to know our own signs and symptoms of cycle phases it can also be nice to start to understand the hormonal changes occurring.

"I'm feeling hormonal" is a common statement we're used to hearing, but what are we trying to communicate when that's said? That we don't feel like ourselves? That we feel like we overreacted about something? That we wish we felt differently? That we are uncomfortable?

Getting to know what you mean when you say you "feel hormonal" can help you further express yourself and validate your emotions. And just because hormones can feel like an explanation of an emotion doesn't make the emotion itself invalid. Becoming mindful of hormone fluctuation can help make sense of mood swings, sensitivities, and emotional needs.

Hormones

When we talk about fluctuations throughout a cycle we are more specifically taking about hormones fluctuating. There are many hormones in the body, but the two we will focus on is estrogen and progesterone.

This visual example is meant to give a sense of what hormone changes occur throughout a cycle. Not all levels look like this for every person during every cycle, but on average one can expect the below changes to occur.

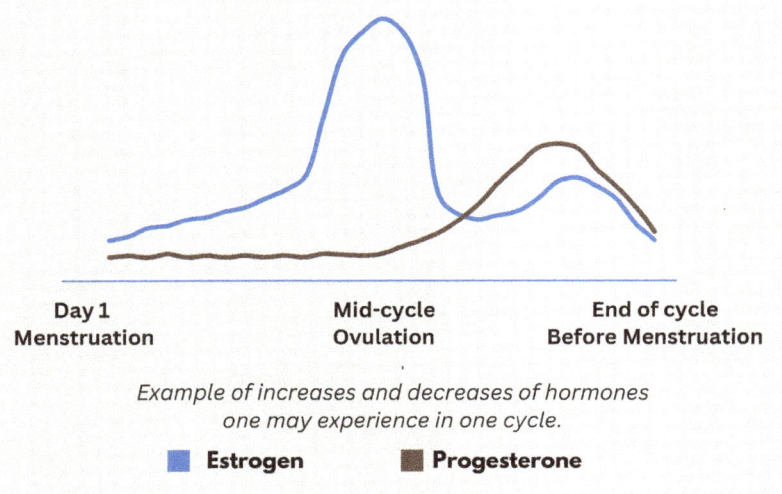

| Day 1 | Mid-cycle | End of cycle |
| Menstruation | Ovulation | Before Menstruation |

*Example of increases and decreases of hormones
one may experience in one cycle.*

■ **Estrogen**   ■ **Progesterone**

Relationship of hormones

While people often talk about hormone levels, the ratio of estrogen and progesterone levels is also important to consider. For example, estrogen dominance occurs if estrogen levels are higher relative to progesterone levels in the last two weeks of the cycle. While you can think of this as having "high estrogen", looking at the bigger picture might show low progesterone impacting this relational imbalance.

Estrogen

Estrogen is associated with the first half of the cycle, it rises in preparation of ovulation which happens mid-cycle. Research suggests that estrogen and serotonin likely interact with regard to mood and affect in both animals and in humans, and could serve as a compounding mechanism by which estrogen influences emotion. Estrogen is also present in the second half of the cycle and is accompanied by progesterone.

Progesterone

Progesterone is a hormone dominant in the second half of the cycle that increases as a result of ovulation occurring. It is considered a "calming" hormone that is meant to support slowing down. If no pregnancy occurs after ovulation, progesterone decreases and the cycle moves into menstruation. People have varying sensitivities to progesterone so not everyone experiences the supportive nature of the hormone. Factors such as one's mental health, stress levels, age, genetics, and childhood trauma are found to have an impact on one's sensitivity to progesterone.

Girdler, S. S., Leserman, J., Bunevičius, R., Klatzkin, R. R., Pedersen, C. A., & Light, K. C. (2007). Persistent alterations in biological profiles in women with abuse histories: Influence of premenstrual dysphoric disorder. Health Psychology, 26(2), 201-213. https://doi.org/10.1037/0278-6133.26.2.201

Kuehner, C., & Nayman, S. (2021). Premenstrual Exacerbations of Mood Disorders: Findings and knowledge gaps. Current Psychiatry Reports, 23(11). https://doi.org/10.1007/s11920-021-01286-0

Sundström-Poromaa, I., Comasco, E., Sumner, R. L., & Lüders, E. (2020). Progesterone - Friend or foe? Frontiers in Neuroendocrinology, 59, 100856. https://doi.org/10.1016/j.yfrne.2020.100856

Wharton, W., Gleason, C. E., Sandra, O., Carlsson, C. M., & Asthana, S. (2012). Neurobiological underpinnings of the estrogen - mood relationship. Current Psychiatry Reviews, 8(3), 247-256. https://doi.org/10.2174/157340012800792957

intersection of mental health

A person's mental health
encompasses one's emotional,
psychological, and social well-
being. Even if someone doesn't
meet criteria for a clinical
mental health diagnosis, one's
mental health can still ebb and
flow with one's cycle. Whether
it be feelings of depression or
spikes of anxiety, people
usually feel different depending
on where they are at in their
cycle.

Additionally, there are also
clinical mental health impacts
to consider when discussing
menstruation. If you struggle
with mental health symptoms, it
can be useful to look at these
through a cyclical lens to see
if there are peaks or valleys of
symptoms during certain points
of the cycle.

Menstruation and Mental Health

While many people experience mild mood and energy shifts throughout their cycle, some experience more severe symptoms that impact their mental health.

Premenstrual Syndrome (PMS) is a common occurrence where people experience symptoms like low mood, anger, irritability, or fatigue before their period. This impacts a lot of people with cycles but is not a mental health diagnosis in and of itself.

In this section we'll cover two cyclical occurrences that have more severe impacts on mental health:
- Premenstrual Dysphoric Disorder (PMDD)
- Premenstrual Exacerbation (PME)

It can be hard to discern between mild to moderate to severe mental health symptoms on your own. I recommend using the information in this guide as a first step and to seek out support with a professional to discuss further care as needed.

What to do if you think mental health symptoms are related to your cycle

1.
Reach out for support

Seek support for current mental health symptoms. Whether symptoms are related to your cycle or not, you don't need to wait to find mental heath support. While access to care can be challenging, many areas have sliding scale clinics and/or virtual therapists who practice state-wide and offer accessible care online.

2.
Start tracking

Track mental health symptoms to see when they occur, compare to cycle phases, notice patterns over time (2-3 months). You can use the tracker included in this book or use an app such as Me v PMDD to track symptoms on your phone. There are many tracking options out there, find one that works with your learning style to support making cycle tracking a daily habit.

3.
Befriend symptoms

Try and get to know symptoms in a nonjudgemental way. Notice what is supportive during physically and emotionally difficult times. This can help you anticipate and manage symptoms, and give you space to decide if you would like further clinical support.

PMDD: Premenstrual Dysphoric Disorder

In 2013, diagnostic criteria was formally accepted for PMDD as the first mental health diagnosis in the DSM* to recognize menstrual cycles.

Examples of PMDD symptoms include anger, irritability, feeling on edge or overwhelmed, anxiety, panic attacks, depression, or suicidal thoughts. PMDD symptoms are present in the 10-14 days before menstruation (luteal phase) and may subside 1-2 days after menstruation begins. A distinct characteristic of PMDD is that symptoms repeat cyclically and are not present in the first two weeks of the cycle.

Symptoms of PMDD are more severe than PMS. PMDD is a clinical mental health diagnosis, versus PMS is a description of symptoms that may be unpleasant and uncomfortable but may not more severely impact one's mental health.

If you are in crisis, please reach out for mental health crisis support:

SAMHSA's National Helpline
1-800-662-HELP (4357)

National Alliance on Mental Illness
Call 1-800-950-6264 or Text "Helpline" to 62640

Resources above are for the United States, if outside of the country please reach out to local mental health support.

*DSM, Diagnostic and Statistical Manual of Mental Disorders is the U.S. handbook for health care professionals to provide a mental disorders diagnosis to support patients and inform treatment.

American Psychiatric Association. (2013). Diagnostic and statistical manual of mental disorders (5th ed.). https://doi.org/10.1176/appi.books.9780890425596

PME: Premenstrual Exacerbation

PME is when existing mental health symptoms fluctuate in correlation with the menstrual cycle. This would mean you have symptoms during all cycle phases and those symptoms regularly peak on specific cycle days.

For example, during the two weeks before menstruation, people with a cycle may experience worsening of mental health symptoms of an existing disorder. Others have reported noticing an increase in symptoms the days following ovulation after estrogen drops. This reference to exacerbation means symptoms are present throughout the cycle, but are elevated at specific times. Different than PMDD, PME is not a mental health diagnosis but acknowledgement of it can help one manage existing mental health symptoms.

Some diagnoses that can be impacted by PME include depression, anxiety, OCD, eating disorders, mood disorders, and ADHD. This doesn't mean everyone with a cycle will experience PME, but it is something to be aware to be able to anticipate and care for oneself.

Kuehner, C., & Nayman, S. (2021b). Premenstrual Exacerbations of Mood Disorders: Findings and knowledge gaps. Current Psychiatry Reports, 23(11). https://doi.org/10.1007/s11920-021-01286-0

Mental health support

Steps can be taken in one's daily life to support menstrual mental health. Depending on individualized needs and treatment care preferences, each person will likely take their own journey to find what actions are most accessible and supportive to their symptoms. Below is a general overview of common treatment appraoches:

Plan ahead, anticipating difficult times is a simple yet impactful action one can take. Identifying what supports work for you may take time, but know that slowing down, planning ahead for self care, and leaning into your cycle can help alleviate physical, mental, and emotional challenges.

Lifestyle changes* such as reducing stress and regulating one's nervous systems, eating balanced and nutritious meals, including specific vitamins and supplements, maintaining regular physical movement (while not over exercising), decreasing or eliminating use of alcohol, nicotine, and caffeine, and getting more sleep are important lifestyle changes to consider.

Clinical support can include working with a psychotherapist, psychiatrist, functional medicine doctor, or nutritionist. It Is also good to have routine medical visits with an OBGYN to identify any underlying health problems that could be amplifying one's menstrual cycle.

Medication* can also be considered for treatment for PMDD. Specifically antidepressant medication such as an SSRI (Selective serotonin reuptake inhibitors) from a prescribing physician can be supportive for managing PMDD symptoms.

*Treatment options including lifestyle changes and medication are evidence-based and part of IAPMD's guidelines for PMDD treatment. For more specific instruction on treatment, please visit IAPMD.org

Treatment Options | Premenstrual Dysphoric Disorder | IAPMD. (n.d.). IAPMD. https://iapmd.org/about-pmdd Treatment Guidelines | Evidence-Based Management of Premenstrual Disorders. IAPMD. (n.d.). IAPMD. https://iapmd.org/treatment-guidelines

Note on clinical support

It is important to recognize that not all medical or mental health professionals are trained in menstrual related disorders. The International Association for Premenstrual Disorders (IAPMD) is a resource for individuals and clinicians looking for the most current research and guidance on treatment for evidence-based lifestyle changes, diet and nutrition, medication, and medical care.

The International Association for Premenstrual Disorders (IAPMD) is a not-for-profit organization providing education, support, advocacy, and resources for those affected by Premenstrual Dysphoric Disorder (PMDD) and Premenstrual Exacerbation of underlying disorders (PME).

Our Story | IAPMD. (n.d.). IAPMD. https://iapmd.org/about

mindful moments

While mindfulness may be a
common term nowadays, its value
should not be overlooked. With a
spiritual history, mindfulness
was brought into the medical
field by Jon Kabatt-Zinn who
designed the Mindfulness Based
Stress Reduction program and
studied its effects on chronic
pain.

Since then, mindfulness has been
used to help support issues such
as depression, anxiety, chronic
pain, and hypertension. It is
also popular way people ground
themselves when feeling
overstimulated and disconnected
from daily life.

As we discuss the act of
noticing cyclical changes in
ourselves, it can be useful to
utilize mindfulness practices to
look at these ebbs and flows
with compassion and curiosity.

Tenets of mindfulness

We can move through our days more mindfully in our thoughts and in our sensory experiences. From a menstrual cycle perspective, this can mean checking in with how we feel and doing so with patience, acceptance, and without judgement.

Below are the tenets of mindfulness that can be applied to various parts of daily life:

Non-judging
The act of holding a nonjudgmental stance for those around us and for ourselves.

Patience
Grounding oneself in the present moment rather than striving for experiencing the future.

Beginner's mind
Showing up to the moment with curiosity and wonder, an absence of pressure or expectation to be an expert coming into a situation.

Trust
Getting in tune with instincts, still adhering to ethical morals but while listening and trusting personal instincts within yourself.

Non-striving
Consider what is in front of you in the present moment without a driving pressure to always be wanting more.

Acceptance
Being able to accept the facts of a situation, this doesn't mean giving up on desired change, but rather first processing the present reality.

Letting go
Notice fixation or rumination on things we cannot change. Take steps to let go of attachment to the things we cannot control.

Connecting with the present moment

Below are a few exercises you can try to help connect with the present moment. Please remember, there is no right way to be mindful, it can be as simple as slowly down and taking a breath.

4-7-8 Breathing

Place one hand on your belly and the other on your chest. Breathe in with your belly; the hand on your belly should rise, while the hand on your chest stays still.

Breathe in for 4 seconds, hold for 7 seconds, exhale for 8 seconds, repeat. Use this breathing exercise as a way to allow a moment for yourself to pause and move with intention.

Mindful Eating

Before eating, observe your meal and notice the colors, textures, and smells of the food.

Enjoy food slowly with intention and without multitasking. Focus on the current bite, avoid hurrying to the next one. Move with ease and occasionally pause to re-engage senses.

RAIN Meditation

Practice a meditation. I recommend the RAIN meditation by Tara Brach. This can usually be found online as a recording with guided audio.

RAIN stands for Recognize, Allow, Investigate, Nurture and is a supportive meditation to mindfully engage with difficult emotions we may otherwise be avoiding.

5-4-3-2-1 Sensory Exercise

Name 5 things you can see, 4 things you can feel, 3 things you can hear, 2 things you can smell, 1 thing you can taste.

This can be used as a way to pause and take in your current surroundings and sensory experiences.

menstrual cycle tips

It is important to remember
changing your relationship with
your cycle can take time. A
menstrual cycle is
representative of the last 1-3
months of one's mental and
physical health. This delayed
impact can be hard to relate to
as society encourages us to find
instant gratification whenever
possible.

Befriending your cycle can be a
slow process. Consider each
cycle an opportunity to be
kinder and more compassionate
with yourself.

Care tips included in this
section are intended to be ideas
of ways to care for oneself
throughout the cycle. Please
note some of these tips are
anecdotal recommendations and
are not all evidence-based
treatments. If you are
experiencing moderate or severe
symptoms, please seek care for
individualized needs.

Tip #1 Lean in, not against

Living in a society that rewards productivity can make someone with a cycle feel less valued during low energy, less productive times in their cycle. Accepting a cyclical life means being flexible with yourself and learning how to move with your body instead of pushing through to meet societal expectations.

Leaning into the cycle can show up as small shifts like resting when you are tired and moving when you are energized. It can mean saying no to an event when you need alone time or making plans when you are feeling social. Moving with this ebb and flow can help enable a smoother transition between phases and more acceptance of one's personal needs.

Reflect

What is my current relationship like with my cycle?

What external messages have I received about my cycle from others (society, culture, family, etc.)?

Where areas of myself can I be easier on myself if I think about my life through a more cyclical lens?

Tip #2 Get to know your cycle

You can read every book and listen to every podcast, but no one can tell you how you feel in your own body.

While symptoms and mood patterns can be commonly shared amongst people, you may experience things in your own unique way. Some people love how they feel In their follicular phase, while others come to find they really love their luteal phase and appreciate the dedicated time to reconnect with themselves.

Knowing your cycle and your symptoms can help empower you to find your own flow.

Connect

What aspects of my cycle feel unique to me?

What questions do I have about my cycle that I have been unsure how to ask?

What do I like/enjoy about my cycle? What do I dislike about my cycle?

Tip #3 Validate period pain

While pain should not be thought of as normal (common normal), it is a reality for many people. Period pain can feel like a dull aching or throbbing in the lower abdomen or back, alongside stomach aches or nausea. Cramps are a result of muscles contracting to shed the uterine lining and can last a few days.

For severe pain, heavy periods, or irregular periods, it is best to see a medical professional to check for an underlying medical issue. Documenting pain over time is a useful tool when speaking to clinicians about symptoms and care.

Aside from symptoms indicating a larger medical diagnosis, some attribute common period pain to nutritional deficiencies, processed foods, not enough sleep, being out of sync with the natural circadian rhythm, over exposure to endocrine disruptors, dysregulated nervous systems, and/or high levels of stress.

Validate

What is hardest for me about my cycle?

What signs indicate that my period is coming?

What bothers you most about period discomfort?

Tip #4 Identify ways to take care

When in pain it is best to slow down, move with your cycle, and take care of yourself. If you were sick, would you not rest? Below are examples of ways to support your cycle overall and to support pain. While doing *all of these* isn't realistic, notice if anything small is easy to add to your life.

Supporting menstrual health in general
❑ Stay hydrated
❑ Minimize caffeine and alcohol
❑ Get sunshine; avoid screens right before bed
❑ Minimize stress levels as best as you can
❑ Eat balanced meals with protein; minimize processed foods
❑ Have breakfast with protein (before coffee)

Leading up to period
❑ Take time to connect with yourself
❑ Start to pivot from high intensity workouts to more moderate or slow movement
❑ Honor need for more calories in luteal, lean into balanced meals
❑ Have magnesium and fiber to keep bowel movements regular
❑ Prep meals before period so future you doesn't have to cook

Prior to onset of pain
❑ Anticipate feeling less social the next few days
❑ Enjoy easily digestible, warm meals
❑ Consider having calming herbal teas such as ginger, red raspberry leaf, chamomile, peppermint, as well as green tea which can be good for inflammation
❑ *If you take an over-the-counter pain medication, can plan taking it at first sign of period pain rather than waiting for pain to spike

Care tips included in this section are intended to be ideas of ways to manage and improve menstrual symptoms. Please note these tips are anecdotal and are not all evidence-based.

*Consult a doctor or pharmacist for individualized care and medication use. This tip is a general recommendation for managing pain, this is not medical advice for individualized care.

During pain

❑ Rest, slow down

❑ Take a break from high intensity workouts

❑ Move your body in a restorative way – try yin yoga or look up yoga positions geared towards menstrual discomfort

❑ Say no to things if you're not up for socializing

❑ Continue enjoying calming herbal teas from previous week

❑ Have warm, cooked meals like soups and stews, and eat anti-inflammatory foods that are easy to digest

❑ Soothe uterine muscles with heat (bath/heating pad/hot water bottle)

❑ Orgasming by yourself or with a partner can reduce period pain, as it relaxes muscles and produces dopamine

❑ Massage abdomen and lower back with topical essential oils, such as lavender, clary sage, dragons blood, peppermint, or ylang ylang

Plan Ahead

What things do I want to try next cycle to take care of myself?

What is one thing I can do for myself during premenstrual or menstrual days (alone time, saying no, etc.)?

What can I say to myself to be kinder on challenging days?

Tip #5 Reframe PMS and your period

Periods can be tough to say the least. Physically and emotionally, it can feel like our body is at war with us. Those feelings are all valid, and in no way do I recommend discounting what you're going through.

If possible though, I do recommend being a little kinder to yourself and your body by reframing what a period means. This is a way to practice moving with your body instead of moving against it.

Reframe premenstrual days and your period as a time to:

• Relax
• Press pause
• Slow down
• Set boundaries
• Validate emotions
• Practice saying no
• Reconnect with yourself
• More easily access anger
• Give your body what it needs
• Practice listening to your body
• Be mindful of negative self talk
• Speak your mind (with compassion)
• Take a step back to reflect and ask yourself if there's anything missing right now from your life, this can be a time to reflect on deeper emotions and larger changes you would like to work towards making

PART II

LEARN YOUR CYCLE

intention of this cycle tracker

The goal of this tracker is to shine a light on your individualized menstrual experience. It is designed to highlight changes in mood throughout one's cycle.

The tracker is centered around mental health and is meant for brief self check-ins to make it accessible for daily use. By tracking 2-3 cycles, you will be able to take a step back and reflect on cyclical patterns and fluctuations.

Tracking can provide a shortcut to identify needs, validate emotions, and better understand your mental health. The goal in tracking one's cycle in this way is to help menstruating people move with their cycle and identify ways to best support themselves.

The cycle tracker can be used writing directly in this book or can be printed out separately.

PDF of monthly tracker page is
available for print-friendly download
and can be found on page 58

why not just use an app

Cycle tracking apps are great, I recommend them for a variety of reasons. I have used one for years and continue to use it on my own journey. Apps have many functions for tracking biomarkers and tracking fertility, or simply anticipating the date of your next period.

This tracker however is focused on building an emotional connection with your cycle. In my experience, this connection comes through more when written privately by hand versus in an app. If you flip ahead to the calendar portion, you'll notice the months and days are blank. That is because in this format, your cycle dictates a new "month". Day 1 will not be January 1, February 1, etc. Instead, new pages will be prompted by the first day of your period. It is a subtle shift, but a significant one to support you seeing your cycle through a new lens.

While it can be difficult at first to build the habit of daily tracking, sticking with it can unlock a stronger sense of self and increased self awareness. I have found a couple months of tracking is all you need to notice patterns and new ways to support yourself.

If writing by hand does not resonate for your learning style or how you best express yourself, I recommend checking out apps like Me v PMDD that are designed to track symptoms for menstrual mental health.

how to use this tracker

1. On the first day of your cycle, fill out the Cycle Days and Date information for the whole cycle month view. I recommend filling out the dates and days for the entire month on day 1 – this way you can look ahead and anticipate different phases of your cycle in the weeks ahead.

2. Each day, briefly make notes on how you feel. This can include mood/emotions, physical state, symptoms, mental health changes, doing/feeling something out of the ordinary, etc. You can even note when you feel shifts and feel like you're in a new phase - for example, when you feel like you're ovulating or when you feel a shift into your pre-menstrual (luteal) phase.

3. At the end of each cycle, start to use the *Reflections* **and** *Intentions* **pages to note more in-depth** takeaways about how you are feeling. You can also use these pages to make notes for a future doctor's appointment or therapy appointment if issues come up during your cycle.

4. After 2-3 months of tracking, start to flip through the tracker and notice patterns that occur in your cycle. While some people track their cycle indefinitely, it is important to note the purpose of this specific tracker is to drop in for a few months as a personal check-in with yourself.

5. The last step will be writing down final *Reflections* **and** *Intentions* **you want to remember moving forward.** Use your judgement on when you feel "done" with monthly tracking, and feel free to note takeaways and "aha" moments throughout the process.

Example

Remember, this tracker is meant to be centered around YOU and YOUR CYCLE. That means each page is blank for you to fill out your cycle days and the current date.

Example if you started your period on Monday, July 3rd

a. Write in Day 1 of your period   b. Write in Calendar date

c. Mark phase you *feel like you're in that week (mark two if you feel like you're in transition)

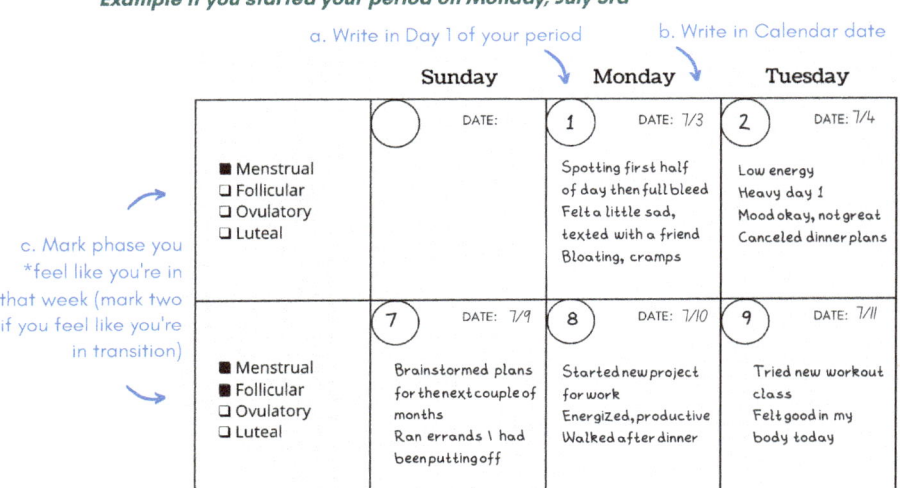

	Sunday	Monday	Tuesday
	DATE:	**1** DATE: 7/3	**2** DATE: 7/4
■ Menstrual ❑ Follicular ❑ Ovulatory ❑ Luteal		Spotting first half of day then full bleed Felt a little sad, texted with a friend Bloating, cramps	Low energy Heavy day 1 Mood okay, not great Canceled dinner plans
	7 DATE: 7/9	**8** DATE: 7/10	**9** DATE: 7/11
■ Menstrual ■ Follicular ❑ Ovulatory ❑ Luteal	Brainstormed plans for the next couple of months Ran errands I had been putting off	Started new project for work Energized, productive Walked after dinner	Tried new workout class Felt good in my body today

Example if you started your period on Wednesday, August 16th

Wednesday	Thursday	Friday	Saturday
1 DATE: 8/16	**2** DATE: 8/17	**3** DATE: 8/18	**4** DATE: 8/19
Slept in Some cramps Did yin yoga before bed Treated myself to ramen	Took it easy at work Cramps in the AM Reset expectations of my day	Starting to physically feel better improved mood, still tired	Finished my period today Medium level energy Mood is regular – not good, not bad
8 DATE: 8/23	**9** DATE: 8/24	**10** DATE: 8/25	**11** DATE: 8/26
Brunch with friends, ran errands, feeling excited for this week	Exercised before work, made plans for later in the week, feeling good overall	Busy day at work felt able to keep up some anxiety today but not too bad – felt burnt out in the evening	Went hiking with friends, Scheduled date night tonight, Gonna dress up

While you can use various biomarkers to track exactly what phase you are in, part of the exercise here is to drop into your emotional and physical experience. This intuitive approach is not meant for family planning, it is meant to encourage each individual to notice their unique experience of each phase.

55

Example of Reflections

I had a hard time trying to rest during my period, I let myself
sleep in more than normal which felt nice. Normally I would
have felt guilty sleeping in but I knew my body needed to rest
so I didn't regret it. My period in general was brutal the first
day/day and a half. I tried some new teas I liked, not sure if
they helped. Using a heating pad was great.

I noticed feeling more social during the follicular/ovulation
days. I dressed up more and made more plans during that
phase to lean into it more. It felt good to take advantage of
having more energy knowing I'd rest soon in my luteal phase.

Example of Intentions

I N T E N T I O N S

I want to take more breaks leading up to my period in my
next cycle. I am going to try scheduling some solo time in for
myself even if its just taking myself to get a coffee one
morning or take a walk after work.

I want to try and validate my PMS more in therapy. I tend to
invalidate my own feelings during that time and I'm curious
how it would be if I honored those feelings more.

What should I remember for tracking?

PDF of monthly tracker is available
for print-friendly download.

Find a time of day that works best for you to
track, and try and make a habit out of it.

Simply note what sticks out to you about each day in regards to
your physical state, mental state, and energy levels.

This tracker is meant to be brief to make it manageable for daily
check-ins. If you have more to say you can expand on reflection pages.

Be kind to yourself. If you miss a day tracking,
that's okay. Try to jump back in and keep going.

CYCLE TRACKER

	Sunday	Monday	Tuesday
❑ Menstrual ❑ Follicular ❑ Ovulatory ❑ Luteal	◯ DATE:	◯ DATE:	◯ DATE:
❑ Menstrual ❑ Follicular ❑ Ovulatory ❑ Luteal	◯ DATE:	◯ DATE:	◯ DATE:
❑ Menstrual ❑ Follicular ❑ Ovulatory ❑ Luteal	◯ DATE:	◯ DATE:	◯ DATE:
❑ Menstrual ❑ Follicular ❑ Ovulatory ❑ Luteal	◯ DATE:	◯ DATE:	◯ DATE:
❑ Menstrual ❑ Follicular ❑ Ovulatory ❑ Luteal	◯ DATE:	◯ DATE:	◯ DATE:

Wednesday	Thursday	Friday	Saturday
DATE:	DATE:	DATE:	DATE:
DATE:	DATE:	DATE:	DATE:
DATE:	DATE:	DATE:	DATE:
DATE:	DATE:	DATE:	DATE:
DATE:	DATE:	DATE:	DATE:

	Sunday	Monday	Tuesday
	DATE:	DATE:	DATE:
❑ Menstrual ❑ Follicular ❑ Ovulatory ❑ Luteal			
	DATE:	DATE:	DATE:
❑ Menstrual ❑ Follicular ❑ Ovulatory ❑ Luteal			
	DATE:	DATE:	DATE:
❑ Menstrual ❑ Follicular ❑ Ovulatory ❑ Luteal			
	DATE:	DATE:	DATE:
❑ Menstrual ❑ Follicular ❑ Ovulatory ❑ Luteal			
	DATE:	DATE:	DATE:
❑ Menstrual ❑ Follicular ❑ Ovulatory ❑ Luteal			

Wednesday	Thursday	Friday	Saturday
DATE:	DATE:	DATE:	DATE:
DATE:	DATE:	DATE:	DATE:
DATE:	DATE:	DATE:	DATE:
DATE:	DATE:	DATE:	DATE:
DATE:	DATE:	DATE:	DATE:

	Sunday	Monday	Tuesday
☐ Menstrual ☐ Follicular ☐ Ovulatory ☐ Luteal	DATE:	DATE:	DATE:
☐ Menstrual ☐ Follicular ☐ Ovulatory ☐ Luteal	DATE:	DATE:	DATE:
☐ Menstrual ☐ Follicular ☐ Ovulatory ☐ Luteal	DATE:	DATE:	DATE:
☐ Menstrual ☐ Follicular ☐ Ovulatory ☐ Luteal	DATE:	DATE:	DATE:
☐ Menstrual ☐ Follicular ☐ Ovulatory ☐ Luteal	DATE:	DATE:	DATE:

Wednesday	Thursday	Friday	Saturday
◯ DATE:	◯ DATE:	◯ DATE:	◯ DATE:
◯ DATE:	◯ DATE:	◯ DATE:	◯ DATE:
◯ DATE:	◯ DATE:	◯ DATE:	◯ DATE:
◯ DATE:	◯ DATE:	◯ DATE:	◯ DATE:
◯ DATE:	◯ DATE:	◯ DATE:	◯ DATE:

	Sunday	Monday	Tuesday
❑ Menstrual ❑ Follicular ❑ Ovulatory ❑ Luteal	◯ DATE:	◯ DATE:	◯ DATE:
❑ Menstrual ❑ Follicular ❑ Ovulatory ❑ Luteal	◯ DATE:	◯ DATE:	◯ DATE:
❑ Menstrual ❑ Follicular ❑ Ovulatory ❑ Luteal	◯ DATE:	◯ DATE:	◯ DATE:
❑ Menstrual ❑ Follicular ❑ Ovulatory ❑ Luteal	◯ DATE:	◯ DATE:	◯ DATE:
❑ Menstrual ❑ Follicular ❑ Ovulatory ❑ Luteal	◯ DATE:	◯ DATE:	◯ DATE:

Wednesday	Thursday	Friday	Saturday
◯ DATE:	◯ DATE:	◯ DATE:	◯ DATE:
◯ DATE:	◯ DATE:	◯ DATE:	◯ DATE:
◯ DATE:	◯ DATE:	◯ DATE:	◯ DATE:
◯ DATE:	◯ DATE:	◯ DATE:	◯ DATE:
◯ DATE:	◯ DATE:	◯ DATE:	◯ DATE:

	Sunday	Monday	Tuesday
☐ Menstrual ☐ Follicular ☐ Ovulatory ☐ Luteal	◯ DATE:	◯ DATE:	◯ DATE:
☐ Menstrual ☐ Follicular ☐ Ovulatory ☐ Luteal	◯ DATE:	◯ DATE:	◯ DATE:
☐ Menstrual ☐ Follicular ☐ Ovulatory ☐ Luteal	◯ DATE:	◯ DATE:	◯ DATE:
☐ Menstrual ☐ Follicular ☐ Ovulatory ☐ Luteal	◯ DATE:	◯ DATE:	◯ DATE:
☐ Menstrual ☐ Follicular ☐ Ovulatory ☐ Luteal	◯ DATE:	◯ DATE:	◯ DATE:

Wednesday	Thursday	Friday	Saturday
DATE:	DATE:	DATE:	DATE:
DATE:	DATE:	DATE:	DATE:
DATE:	DATE:	DATE:	DATE:
DATE:	DATE:	DATE:	DATE:
DATE:	DATE:	DATE:	DATE:

PART III

NEXT STEPS

reflections

Reflect on your relationship with your cycle and on your experience tracking. You can use time to reflect during each menstrual phase or wait until the end of tracking a couple cycles to reflect.

Below are some examples of prompts to reflect on either in discussion with someone or in writing for personal self reflection.

Reflections

- *How did it feel tracking my cycle?*

- *What was hard? What was enjoyable?*

- *Is there a phase I feel most comfortable in?*

- *Is there a phase or specific cycle days that are most challenging for me?*

- *Did I notice connections between my cycle and my mental health?*

- *Did I discover new ways to support myself?*

- *In what ways has my relationship with my cycle changed since I started this process?*

REFLECTIONS

REFLECTIONS

REFLECTIONS

REFLECTIONS

REFLECTIONS

REFLECTIONS

intentions

Take some time to set intentions about how want to care for and support yourself based on what you learned in this process.

Consider some of the examples below of prompts for intentions to set in discussion with someone or in private for personal self reflection.

Intentions

- *Are there new ways I want to lean in more to specific cycle phases?*

- *What has been most supportive for me on difficult days that I want to continue?*

- *Are there times I want to communicate to a partner, family member, or friend when I need support/space?*

- *Are there specific aspects of my cycle I want to continue to track?*

- *Are there specific aspects of my cycle I want to discuss with a doctor, therapist, or other health professional?*

INTENTIONS

INTENTIONS

INTENTIONS

INTENTIONS

INTENTIONS

INTENTIONS

moving forward

You can continue to track your cycle in many different ways. Below are some things to consider when thinking about next steps for yourself and your tracking:

Options for future tracking

- *Continuing to track by hand: Offers emotional connection to what day of your cycle you are on and what that day/phase means to you.*

- *Using an app: Offers a range of benefits and are popular for fertility tracking (both when trying to conceive and also when trying to not conceive.) Some apps can even track Body Basil Temperature (see page 12) when synced to wearable technology. Options are endless really. Popular apps are Natural Cycles, MyFlo, and Clue. The best app out there is the one you enjoy using!*

- *Seasons of tracking: I find people go in and out of tracking depending on their life stage. I recommend finding what feels right to you for your current needs and be open to trying something new if it's useful.*

- *Tracking for PMDD: For more in-depth PMDD resources, IAPMD offers a variety of options for clinical symptom tracking.*

- Note from Joanna -

My hope is that this guidebook helps you develop a stronger and more positive relationship with your cycle and your mental health.

It was important to me to keep this book brief and mental health focused. If you are looking for other resources or other speciality areas there are many incredible people publishing research, books, and other content for menstrual health. I'll included some recommendations here and I encourage you to keep learning about your body as much as it feels nourishing and supportive to do so.

Thank you to everyone who helped with this labor of love. You know who you are and I greatly appreciate you.

- Additional Resources -

Wild Power
Sjanie Hugo Wurlitzer and Alexandra Pope

You Can Have a Better Period: A Practical
Guide to Pain-free and Calmer Periods
Le'Nise Brothers, Registered Nutritionist

Period Repair Manual: Natural Treatment for
Better Hormones and Better Periods
Dr. Lara Briden, N.D.

Menopause Bootcamp: Optimize Your Health,
Empower Your Self, and Flourish as You Age
Dr. Suzanne Gilberg-Lenz

International Association For
Premenstrual Disorders
iapmd.org